W9-ACD-610

The Sacred Seasons

ams press
new york

PS
3503
.O164
S3
1975

The Sacred Seasons

poems by

Carl Bode

DALE H. GRAMLEY LIBRARY
SALEM COLLEGE
WINSTON-SALEM, N. C.

Denver, **ALAN SWALLOW,** *1953*

Library of Congress Cataloging in Publication Data

Bode, Carl, 1911-
    The sacred seasons: poems.

    Reprint of the 1953 ed. published by A. Swallow, Denver,
in series: The New poetry series.
    I. Title.
[PS3503.O164S3   1975]   811'.5'4   75-179807
ISBN 0-404-56007-5
        0-404-56000-8 (SET)

The New Poetry Series

Reprinted by arrangement with
The Swallow Press Inc.
Copyright © 1953 by Alan Swallow
First AMS edition published in 1975
AMS Press Inc. 56 E. 13th St.
New York, N.Y. 10003

Manufactured in the USA

To Arthur Nethercot

CONTENTS

No Elegies At All

The Sacred Seasons

I

Stained by black light and smeared
By blood oozing from stone
Know the hot ambiguity of being alone
As it fulfills what you wantonly feared.
Know that the tower wants most to be taken.
The flesh crawls to leave the bone
And even in the midst of most pious moan
The cause pleads to be forsaken.

The stone smashing, the blood comes black
While by infinite and planned regress
You delicately go back and back,
Back to the God who will blast not bless,
Whom you will sacrifice on bloody stone—you,
Consummate then in being purely wrong, wholly
    untrue.

ADVENT SEASON

The icy lake beyond the birthing
Chills even the brightest death
And it is such a death we are
Unearthing under the sexton's frosty breath.

The dirt is neatly shoveled—
Fire has warmed the clay—
And there where a verger slipped and
Groveled a surer man will today.

He is going now through a travail
Which promises a quick coming here,
Where the bright lake grips the
Gravel, with never a mound to rear.

So we huddle in bleak expectation
And wait for the body to be borne
Arched in a long summer night's
Invitation now, now when its membranes are torn.

The splendid arc of fishnet cast wide upon the sea
Involves no school; the subtle fish stay free.
The cords reticulate the water in inter-angled swells,
With brown lines patterning over the stately wells.
The men who man the boat refuse to understand
That of the oaken boat submerged by sand
Only the sheathed bottom and the ribs are left.
They stare; they wonder of what they are bereft.

That net was cast by no one; yet who is really free?
The net, itself surrounded, all too soon will be
Twisted, torn of cordage, warped, and ragged of weft;
And though the flashing fish are dialectic, swift, and
    deft
They still will gasp upon the sand—within the sunken
    boat—
While the torpid fishers of men hold freedom by the
    throat.

Feast of Saint Andrew the Apostle

You gather that the age unlocks its stone
To stare at it with yellow birdlike eyes
And see the sterile strength with no surprise.
This age, this ostrich age, seems not too wise.
You feel that time crawls forward to atone
For intercostal sins committed in disguise
So that all too many a fissure lies
Over the vanished heart and within the bone.

Well, let the bone soften in the sun, bit by bit.
Cry triumph. Write in the calcareous slime
The traditional commonplaces about time.
Then not looking back know that piercing it
Will rise the spikes of a tremendous ancient claw,
Dun phoenician threat to error and to law.

Feast of Saint Thomas the Apostle

DALE H. GRAMLEY LIBRARY
SALEM COLLEGE
WINSTON-SALEM, N. C.

V

Should I return that orient star and place
It in the yet illumined ranges of the mind?
I promise with a word that its steel glint will blind
The eyes of wisdom's jocund, ugly face.
Lady, it is enough for you to trace
The flutes of light down toward the true and kind
And so stab the eye with light many-tined,
Pin-pointed; and make blindness a lonely grace.

Then shall we see white wisdom put forth his hand
And with faltering, shuffling steps walk toward
The star, while you and I in absolute accord
Look at one another and never dare suspect
That his arm reaches out not to seek, to understand,
Or learn, but to fend off and to reject.

Feast of the Nativity of Our Lord

VI

Cold the coarse mastiff and the person still,
Blued and battered beyond the trite recall
Of any apostate bugle that in the hall
Has hung tarnished instead of being blown on the hill.
Pelts torn, the bloods have mingled and encrust
    beneath
The walker with the red armband and the litter
Who now jolts along with short step and bitter
But hides within the kennel the dry wreath

So that at the proper time there may be interred
Instead, in casque blithe with hunting and sad
With scroll inscribed in gilt with the Word,
Whatever is left of customary good or bad
In the weight of mastiff whom the slain person had,
Before it leapt on him sullenly, never even heard.

Feast of Saint Stephen, Deacon and Martyr

13

Sleep late. Who wants a future like ours to gauge?
The morning turns like any tortured star.
All spent are dawns of myrrh and cinnabar
And pendant time is empty even of its rage.
All that it now dare ask is to assuage
The long weals that torment it and that scar
Its coming, black as the mountains are,
And promise to smolder on for many an age.

Sleep late. Close all the wide windows of the mind—
Compared with the day to come this dawn is kind.
So never see the mountains writhe and reach
Nor the cities stand like children, blind and small
Looking up at the sky, holding each to each.
No, spend one peaceful sigh and turn to the wall.

Feast of the Holy Innocents

VIII

NOT FIRE NOR SWORD
NOR ANY IN BETWEEN

Fire is best of all. Burnt clean and white
Utterly bare my love will walk in state
Over hills and towers, will desolate
All who view her among the concourse of the night.
Before her will bow the whisperings the bright
Rustlings of air, about her will attend a spate
Of ebony dreams, above her will corruscate
Only one the most silver most pointed light.

The long hours of lying on silk are burnt away.
Grave and complete staring straight ahead
My love walks now. And I stand still and grey.
Fire is best—but I have never even dared the sword.
Yet I, I see her stop, tilt back her head,
Look at the lone light, and follow it to an eastern
    Lord.

Feast of the Epiphany

With placid morning face of one most sure of love
You are to rise and move across the brightened room
To where I stand still, letting only light illume
The long staircase of the columns and the dove;
And I must see one flower velvet and purple on the
     lawn below
And idly ask, What is that flower, how long will it
     bloom?
Then I shall forget its austere richness and faint
     perfume
While I await you, for you are all I live to know.

And never believe that the moments while I wait
Are better than the sentient moment when you reach
     my side;
Yet through your touch, caryatid Time will have me
     terrified
Into looking out beyond the lawn, beyond the wine-
     dark sea.
—Years later I shall stop a moment, hesitate,
And learn the flower was amaranth and was for me.

Feast of the Conversion of Saint Paul

X

INDWELLING

This in a house of cupolas, a room for bombasin:
Through the beaded doorway and before a marble
    fireplace
I thought I saw your hand drawn down your own
    face.
Touching the silken smoothness of the skin
Your fingers followed the fair surface in
And then it came to me that what they felt alone
Was underneath, was the austere incorruptible bone.
I stared at where the mirror should not have been.

The gaslight flickered on the mantel, and your eyes
Attended your hand with sad and knowing surprise.
The livid mirror flawed its cheeks and lips.
How could I tell that your tangent fingertips
Though soft like those of casual Magdalen
Tore at what was far beneath the bone, and far within?

Feast of the Purification of Saint Mary the Virgin

17

LENTEN SEASON

The oily smell of life everlasting clings
To all it touches.
The black pool poured upon the sunken grave
Gleams as it smudges.

Above the grave the tree-bound birds
Are supposed to sing
Instead of flying cursively away
On blackened wing.

But warned by the odor of eternity
They soon will go—
Sensible, mechanical, they see that
What is so is so.

Only man stays to survive, staring down
At the oily pool,
Never letting die
Its dark, iridescent, dual
Gilding by the sky.

XII

EASTERTIDE

Oh stupid miracle of my own devising,
To be seen in spite of soot flakes floating down,
Spring shall be here—only through my arising
Into this deadened town.

The last snow in the street has just dried away,
Leaving its little drifts of dirt behind.
The squares of lawn before each house are grey
And the windows are blind.

Shortly, some people will come to look for me;
But, till now, the only sign of life anywhere
Has been some chimney smoke rising quietly
Into the vacant air.

Now, having lain in a cellar three blank days,
I arise. But it is my own new life I put
Into the renascent town ... My own face greys
Under the last flecks of soot.

XIII

Mind's Eye

In what invasion did you die?
Were you splintered upon the adamantine sun?
And what shock sharded the many mind?
Was this the one?

If this was it, take courage.
See the convolvulus climbing up the wall
Toward the smashed stones that no one
Notices at all.

Heavy with the dust of early sunshine
The pretty vine, you may be sure, will pick
Its dainty way, twining loverlike
Between the cold thick

Fragments, and reaching in to
Curl about your fractured mind,
Grow over your bland eyes and leave
Them more than blind.

This invasion has just begun. Unseen,
The shattered casket of no triune thought
Contains the stones' most floral wisdom
Convulsed and caught.

XIV

What does the beast clawing and trifling portend?
Only a few scratches at the throat
Predict conclusions far off and too remote
To make your stiff-necked and righteous bend
Their heads to peer at vulgate type or send
Green shudders in a long black coat
Up to the pulpit; instead they will devote
Their energies to ways they comprehend.

But soon the vacant pulpit will be filled
By a keen and tawny minister of war
Yearning toward the scarlet pews now stilled
Where all the righteous rustled in before.
He will lean forward and lick his lips of blood,
Then discourse to the drowned upon the Flood.

Feast of the Nativity of Saint John Baptist

Of aging and the change that teazes time
Your ruined mountains and crumbled cliffs can tell
Yet you have seen it demonstrated well
By an infant corpse half covered with white lime.

One fall you slept through till the hour of prime
In some convent grounds that cover a whole city block;
You awoke numb but with a growing sense of shock
To see yourself half hidden with frost and rime.

Above the midmost mountain you stood with alpen-
stock
A fancy climber gravelled without his guide;
Eyes dull, you peered into the white of pride
But could not find the rock of Peter the Rock

Although the astonied bishop stopped here with staff
in hand
Above the lines of burning crosses on the desert sand.

Feast of Saint Peter the Apostle

XVI

Have you walked in the night with firm tread
Only to step on the outstretched hand
Of a friend lying sprawled on the wet sand,
Slipped and almost dropped beside her, but instead
Recovered with a gasp; and down on the dead
Turned a face wiped of all emotion and bland?
Then, calm with relief, have you paused to stand
And smile at tears that others will later shed?

I myself would have dropped to my knees
And heaped up sand over her. I would have played
The child, smoothing the mounds, slow, undismayed,
Stopping to hear the warm benighted seas.
I would at least, everyone understands,
Have stopped to cross her bright and beatific hands.

Feast of Saint Jude the Apostle

The Portland Elegies

TIME OF MAN

When: the long ribbons of the wind, the wind
Trailing in ribbons; the day undisciplined,
Knowing no forgiveness; the people hurrying
And looking straight ahead; you, my father,
Elbowing your way through the dead, the
Known dead. Never let me stop you, you
Who see time as an iron bar breaking the
Knees; push your way through the wind as
You wish; let the women feel the day driving
Them, their whipt backs bare, their hair
Fluttering over their eyes in disease; stand
Next to me, my father, my kind; you and
I, only, can stride through the dividing
Days, you and I, both blind: now: blind.

THE MAUSOLEUM AT PORTLAND: I

Their faces wide and hard the angels have read
The stone its letters blurred blue with grime
And the workings of all weather in time
The light must fade and what the letters said
In words or wings may not again be read
How long will angels stare at stones
When will they rise and call to me these bones
In uncorrupted flesh angels can soon imbed
With the deftness of the dreamer or the dead
But still the angels wait and it may be
Always shall while the heavy room around me
Contracts itself to kill the granite walls
Embracing me prove what the angels read
Not only I but they themselves are dead

THE MAUSOLEUM AT PORTLAND: II

In the hardest light of the sun the stone angels shall sadly stand until the antichrist is come to rule over his promised land.

Then will the goat and fox grow fat upon our breast, and day and night make a double beast with East and West, while the hymeneal chants arise into a rite and our great Juan's eyes swell with his cursed spite.

We all will be made to sing that all is for the best.

Then, then—at the loudest noise—a marble wing shall move above.

Angels shall topple on us as we die for love.

So. They and I are back from the outside.
Sitting in the cold sunlight of the parlor
We agree, with no pride,
That we never saw so many lovely flowers.
Petals still lie on the rug; the heavy scent has not died.

There is not much else for us to talk
About really—not much to say or do,
Except to get up and walk
Around in the cold, scented sunlight; so I sit
Looking down, and pull into strands a piece of
flower stalk.

I think, of course, of that night last year
When I dreamt that you need not have died, so that
my
Mind was filled with a dull, queer
Kind of loneliness which would not go away for
A long while; I remember it well as I sit here.

And I well remember those flowers,
Thick leaves with dust on them, coarse hairy stems
Forced by late summer showers.
The blooms were large and had a flat, metallic
Odor. They were bouquets of love, they were ours.

Not just in Elis, but across the vales
Of Arcady, some ragged furrows run;
Where shepherds piped beneath a satin sun
Before, they now dig trenches in the dales.
The hungry sheep look up and are not fed
Before the pastoral butchering has begun.
At last they try, but only try, to run.
Above the eastern hill towers a tortured head.

The shepherds hope for merely phantom fleets
And stop their digging to crane at the sky.
Night comes, and with it talk of matial feats.
But slowly, one by one, the shepherds deign,
Amid embastioned hills, to look east—in vain—
For Bedlam's star to teach them how to die.

Flying aloft in circles, circles the mighty Word.
Swift wreaths of phospor light
Anneal the howling night while we tremble
At any bird.

We curvet backward craning, then bow into a front
Shuddering at a barnyard hawk
And we strain in fearful gawk at its
Unplunging hunt.

The preying bird destroys us and never swoops at all;
We end in a flash of fright;
While up above, thrice given,
The Word by now has driven
The shrieking heaven bright and is
Unnoticed as we fall.

Shining, the shaft of dust is warm and soft
Yet stricter than light alone;
Not kindling to supple youth,
Not cold though to a crone.

Waiting in the attic of the afternoon,
Late afternoon, here naved
Rises recollection's trunk-filled church
For the ragtags you have saved.

Old woman worn beyond decision,
Nod to the slanting pillar of dust.
See that it leads toward one trunk more,
In the corner. See that it must.

A trunk with silver handles, within which
One must lie
And hide grey hairs and hide
Old bones in wrappings made of sky.

The cancer of the mind might be cut out
By a swift surgeon's steel, new tissue planted,
So that you could walk strong and demented
Seeing nothing in the world to cringe about.
Or, better, the knife could cut too close.
That would be reason for bumbling laughter.
Thus surely you would not need thereafter
Even to stalk around, mindless and gross.

Try either: you have no other choice. Be sure
To remember, alleviation must begin,
And end, always end as well, within
Just like each paroxysm you endure.
This is no disease better than its cure,
And the surgeon is still you. Lay the knife in!

Sit in the sun and dry your hair.
Remind me of the dandelion,
Strong, yellow, bitter, and fair.

I will forget a lady who sat
Before a lavendar mirror and smoothed
Dark curls under a tricorne hat.

Put on thick sandals and trudge with me
Through the sand dunes, among the grass
Down to the blunt and bustling sea.

Then I will think I have never known
A curtained room in a cottage where
The noise of the sea was just a moan.

Breast with me the clashing wave
And let it flood the tiny sound
Of a shrouded lady lying alone,
A lady whom merely air has drowned.

Somberly led to aisles of stone, the waters mock
The child by changing to bitter blue,
By flattening under ice, by wearing old anew
And letting waves be turned to guileful rock;
Yet better this reply to the staring child than shock
And waves' concussion when waters wreak
A still revenge on their disclosers and seek
The long columnar quiet of level in a lock,

Fearing the child will plumb those depths to find
By its own seeking the end of life and mind,
Even with eyes observing that heavy waters alone
Can ever let soft plains of stonedust drift
In answer down to the bottom and there shift
In patterns, to form the new and solid stone.

Perhaps the sky is burning
After the outrageous night
But there is no warmth returning in
Its bleak light

The night is best forgotten
If such can ever be
Let it submerge and rotten in the
Corruptive sea

Only a watery flame
Now kindles the early sky
And only man is to blame when
Burnt men die.

Yet all the angels now
With a sweep of trailing claws
Embrace the blackened bodies,
And love the cause.

How green the green at Salem is,
The lawn below the sea,
So lay a lace upon the face,
The face no longer his
Nor like to be,

A gauze upon the curious gaze
And then in sea-green fear
At the trees bent over the lawn
Let him go his curious ways,
Or far or near,

To the richness of the water. Why,
Peace has never been here.
Yet who can say where it has gone?
Who has seen it disappear?

THE GOOD EARTH

He lies who says there are no saints on earth—
Lies or is blind or ignorant as a beast.
But who proclaims the cross? As best
The scrawny bigot
Rooting the red clay for his saving.

The rushing April rain washes over the red
Clay hills and floods all greenery
Away, leaving the ugly farms
Sterile and the one
Dirty town naked with animals.

Yet there are a few saints. I even know
More than one. But most of us: sows
Defending—or devouring—what we
Beget; malicious hens;
Dogs mounting
Each other at the street corner;

Celebrating spring on red mud farms or muddy
Streets. Lord Jesus, what is there,
What can you see, in most of us
To make us
Worth the saving?

No Elegies At All

MEA CULPA

All aids has the animal, within, of pride:
Bile, self-love, blood, casuist wit.
Yet am I his hell? Or is he out of it
Now when his yellow eyes alight on me inside
The iron garden, impaled on the iron fence,
And widen to watch me whisper through the spikes,
Whisper— as the first of the lightning strikes—
To the last remaining angel, Get thee hence?

I have been somewhat more of fool than knave—
And even to that the animal assents,
Adding that this admission is truly brave
And shows a fine acknowledgment of sin.
So, fool to fool, pretense upon pretense,
I see the animal loll again within.

VARIATION ON THE THEME OF
SWEENEY

The hothouse grapes are plainly marked for sale;
Rank purple and luxuriant they invite
Perspiring buyers to stop, taste, and avail
Themselves of jungles— and to stay the night.
But torpid vines above deny their subtle vendor
Though arching over the bowers of the sky;
The fruit they hold is characterized as tender
Only by the fat unspeakable passerby

Who merely wants to cheapen a vixen for a pet
But pauses to survey the dark enlaced domain
Of love with stupid eyes or even better yet
Enters the sated stillness to explain
That purchased mind will weep within the heart,
Tears salt the grapes, and love tear love apart.

THE STUDENT

I have lain in the dirt with bruised imprinted head
To feel nothing but the blackness of cold pain
And I have waited outside myself, dead, in the rain
Recalling too late what the defaced instructions said.

The sinuous swirls of music, the awkward elegance of
        type
Combine to tempt the raveller who should await
        instead
Thumbs at his throat, with finger nails of red,
That burst the swelling skin like a plum far over-ripe.

Now, though. I admit, the history of the ablative
Compiled by the fatal scholar at night will wipe
Out most memories of spectacles, wet lips, and pipe;
But let no one ever ask himself, What have I to give?

O shall we celebrate with learned and pious grace
The green shadows cast by a dead face?

Avoid me. I prefer to cross the street
Having peered both ways for traffic and walk
On the shadowed side. We might have to talk
Otherwise and our eyes might have to meet.
I would have to squint up to the sun and heat—
And a spasm shuts my eyes at the mere thought.
How could I escape feeling overbound and caught?
What could I mewl in answer, by your feet?

The mystic soars above the skies in splendor,
Determines and transcends the very sun
And in the fierce victory of surrender
White bright and blind he melts in the Mystic One.
I myself dread all communion, having died
Whenever I could not cross the street to the other side.

A crooked glow of sagebrush for longer hills
Or vales deciding how the night might send
Annealing lines of fire to world and to world's end
Dares us to ask in absence, Who is it wills
Such fiery, grinding mills, Palestinian mills?
If known, let him be killed in little, let him be arched
In most lasting thirst, fed on dry meal and parched,
And then let him be cooled by an air that kills.

Far cast and azure centered, no skies should leave
The sky; for even Babylonian faith in heat
May make a desert sun too drily incomplete;
And the last way of action may first need to deceive
Sagebrush, the hills and vales, the idea of Palestine—
Leaving only the fiery word, Be mine, be mine.

The great black bust of Minerva, head too large
For its shoulders, stands on an ivory pedestal.
The pedestal is cracked but leans against a
Plaster wall. Behind Minerva stretch dull
Vistas of golden oak down the hall—but who
Can see all the way down the hall? Only a fool
Can be sure there are rooms at the end of the
Hall— rooms half lit, dark in the corners,
With galleries of golden oak far above the eyes.
And books piled on the floor and shelved in dim
Rows in the galleries. And dust. Dust, brown
On the books,

                grey on minerva, softly capping her
Helmet, resting on her shoulders, caught on her
Heavy breasts. And there it rests. There it rests.

UNCLE KARL

Luminal vast and sadly unattended
The plenitude of the moon challenged revoked
Like a heavy workman laid by the splendid
Apron and joked but dialectically joked
About the orange on its shrubby bush being poked
In with lambent joy and pecked at by cockatoos
Whose subconscious had reactionary views
That the waning light of history soon uncloaked

Deep in the British Museum the ideologue has sat
Haloed by the waxing moon and aproned in angry fat
With a sorry dog half crouched upon his shoulder
Dog livid of eye and maw to put the night to shame
Who bays at the lunar kingdoms that
They and their orange moon must bear the blame.

(It begins) Gather the spear into the palm
Exactly as an old book shall try to direct
You, and the torn hand will lead you into the calm
Crumbling church which only the good neglect.
It dares demand the intoning of a psalm
Of wickedness even to music by the self-elect.
For them, remember your hurt hand and Gilead's
    balm.
Then bow, but in cruciform. And recollect

That all too soon the sun will shine through glass
Upon two lines of marble residents
Whose bones have long dispersed in dust.
O Romans, your own bodies will not pass
Unless the rolling thunder of the mount assents.
As to the blooded spear, hang it up—it will not rust.

Within yet far above me the cobalt oceans rise.
On their mountain peaks of bursting white
Their thunder trembles, height on height
Waiting to drown mankind's pandemic cries,
While most of me determines with polite surprise
The politics of atoms or spends the night
Numbering grains of sand, weighing spume of light
Or matching the tints of cobalt with the skies.

For I maintain that it is surely love of learning
When the impending waters curl to a vast concave
That helps one to ignore their slow and inward
    turning;
Though measured knowledge drown within assured
    and brash
I learn that less than bravery can make man brave
So let idea engulf me when the waters crash!

THIS TIME

Speak to the devil and when he nears
Pat him like a dog; scratch him along the back
Of his enormous neck and pull his pointed ears.
Praise him; do not mind that little fleck
Of foam he shows. Ignore the eye rolled backward
And the ponderously accelerating breath;
For there are many things more awkward
Than the awkwardness of death.

If need be. let him lick your skull
And linger in the corners where there once
Were eyes. All this will be much less than dull
Since you are apt to sicken for many months.
But then will be born again, again will rise—
To flatter the evil dog beneath your riven skies.

Monday then, and the sullen throne and angry door
Wait in the drifts of sunlight. Who can defend
Imperial purple when all other colors contend
To form the question, What are they waiting for?
These quiet noises, ransacking the week, stay to abhorr
You, while you are repelled by the odor that tamarind
(Having a pulp, used for preserves, and tawny-
    skinned),
Tree of fruit, gives when laid upon your floor.

Monday then; and more, much more, since the flattest
    dust
Prays for the time to grind against your soul,
To rise and jet rock against you. You must
Not need the shouting rebel— the angry room
The hating dust, these are enough. The many-armed
    assume
The godhead. Do not go in. The parts anatomize the
    whole.

Into the flamboyant cavern of the lonely screen
You, heavy and middle-aged, may always wander;
So exile the garish afternoon, and in you blunder.
Beyond the dim electric torches Life is ready to be
    seen,
Life where no one need ask, What does this mean.
Where two foredestined hearts will never stay asunder.
Here you will be ravished by romance; amid recorded
    thunder
Its enormous kiss will smear you with saccharine.

This is the marriage; clutch your ticket stub. Now
    yield
To him, the husband once-removed . . . And now the
    torches flare,
And now, to seek in many a less than technicolored
    field
For Prince Aeneas, Queen, you slowly forth must fare.
You may seem satiate enough and given to clerks, not
    books,
But glance yourself at the exit and know how Dido
    looks.

REMARKS ABOUT ART: I

I am the one who sits in the front seat
By the driver; and, as we veer toward
The headlong cars, I press on the floorboard,
Braking with no brake. But it is no matter.
Many times I have felt the last shocked beat
Of blood through the windshield's stunning shatter.
We who have suffered frequent translation
Fear too that our death in art is despised.
Since all we dare write is universalized
Into the commonplace, only stagnation,
Immortal, waits; and mechanic creation
Kills those first whom it sees unprized.
For others the burst concussion is disguised;
They lean back, live, inflate with inspiration.

REMARKS ABOUT ART: II

Painted the picture, posed the problem you see.
Strove to study the flat clouds laid on with a knife
But the butcher's taking his wife to wife
Distracted and at length dissuaded me
So I delicately drank of my dish of tea.
And from where I peered the mountains of cloud
As I argued to you looked like a folded shroud.
Liking the brushwork you assented, judicially.
One puts down the teacup, gulping the hot drink.
Who is the painter, no one stops to ask.
I embrace you, or try to, calling art a pure task,
An evil eminence, a fool's fire, a sink.
Shaken and annoyed I envy the butcher his pelf
For the soul has only the soul to portray itself.